Psalms

At His Feet Studies

By Hope A. Blanton and Christine B. Gordon

19Baskets

Psalms: At His Feet Studies
© 2018 by Hope A. Blanton and Christine B. Gordon
ISBN 978-1-946862-07-5

19Baskets, Inc.
PO Box 31291
Omaha, NE 68131
https://19baskets.com

First Edition

Cover design by Sophie Calhoun

Photography by Rebecca Tredway

Contents

At His Feet Story

A few years ago, Hope started looking for materials for the women's fall Bible study at our church. While she found a great number of quality Bible studies, she had a hard time finding studies written for women by women who were reformed. She also had a tough time finding in depth studies of the scripture that didn't take a whole lot of time. In a moment of desperation, Hope asked Chris if she would be willing to co-write a study on Romans, convincing her by asking, "I mean, really, how hard could it be?" And so it began. Weekly emails back and forth, Chris deep in commentaries, Hope mulling over questions, tweaking, editing, asking, pondering. A group of women at Redeemer Presbyterian Church in Lincoln, Nebraska patiently bore with us as we experimented with them every week, and learned to find our rhythm as writers.

Two years later, Hope approached Chris again, softening her up by telling her she could choose any book she wanted. I Samuel it was. Old Testament narrative is the best. Another study was born. About this time, women started asking us for copies of the two studies we had written. While trying to send endless pdfs to people around the country via email, a pastor friend who happens to be a publisher approached Chris and Hope at a party, offering to publish their Bible studies. Suddenly, they had a way to get these into the hands of women who could use them. This had been the point of the whole enterprise – to help make the book of Romans accessible to women. But what would the name be?

During the 1st century, when Jesus walked the earth, a Jewish rabbi would have been surrounded by his students, with some of the men sitting as his feet to learn and listen. This was the custom, the understood norm of the day. But in Luke 10:39, Mary sat at the feet of Jesus. Mary, a woman, was taught by this unconventional rabbi. Mary was given the dignity of taking in his words, his pauses, his tone. She was as worthy of his teaching to Jesus as the men in the room, as are we, his women students today. And so we are At His Feet Bible Studies, hoping to sit at the feet of Jesus while we study his word.

Please find our other available studies at our website:
www.athisfeetonline.com

User Guide

There is no right way to lead a Bible study. Every Bible study group is made up of different types of women with various sets of needs and dynamics. Below are some suggestions that might be helpful when using At His Feet Studies. Read it through. Use what you want. Forget the rest. We're glad you're here.

Participants Guide

This study is laid out like most commentaries. Each chapter is broken up into smaller portions with explanations of the verses in order. There are questions in the chapters before and after the commentary. The first set of questions are Observation Questions designed to help the reader interact with the basic content of the chapter. The second set of questions are Reflection Questions designed to help the reader engage her heart with the text in a vulnerable way.

Start by reading the Scripture passage noted at the top of the study page. Then answer the Observation Questions. Next, go back and read the Scripture side by side with the commentary, pausing between each grouping of verses to absorb both the commentary and the text more deeply. Then move on to answer the Reflection Questions.

Leaders Guide

There are eight questions for each study. When in a group setting, we suggest choosing your favorite Reflection Questions to focus on, especially if you run short on time. If you have more time feel free to work through all the questions. For those groups where people have not had the time and space to read through the commentary and questions, you can simply read the commentary out loud at the beginning of your time. That way all women can participate. We always suggest reading the Scripture passage out loud before you begin.

Extras

The focus verse is something to spend time reflecting on since it's the heart of the passage. Consider memorizing it individually or as a group.

Use the section we have labeled "Reflections, Curiosities, Frustrations" to write down things about the text that seem confusing to you or hard for you to wrap your brain around. This is meant to give you space to express how you're a work in progress as you work through this text and engage with God's Word.

Study 1

On the wall of my bedroom hangs a three-by-four-foot framed poster with 150 images, all neatly aligned in fifteen rows of 10 images each. Included in the collection are photographs of a nurse crouched over a patient in a sickbed, a conductor with arms outstretched to an orchestra in the final crescendo of a symphony, a woman laughing with her eyes closed and mouth open wide, and a helicopter rescuing someone from turbulent waters. There are drawings of a man with a back almost unrecognizable from all of the scars he has gained from lashings, a corrupt politician making promises to a crowd, and a man protecting his refugee child inside his tattered winter coat. Each of these images was chosen to represent the situation, the feelings, the experience described in an individual psalm. The Psalms are poetry and song, yes, but they are not dry, dusty, distant lyrics from unfamiliar scenes. They are real prayers by real people for real life. They are born out of distress and longing, joy and relief, desperation and grief. They are given to us from the one by whom we are "fearfully and wonderfully made" (Psalm 139:14), full of these varied, powerful emotions. Far from telling us to ignore these feelings, the Psalms give us words to pray them. In fact, "when sung in faith, they actually shape the emotions of the godly."

Where did the Psalms come from? How did this collection of 150 separate psalms come to be? Unlike other books in the Bible written by a single author, this book includes songs written by Asaph, Solomon, Moses, David, and the sons of Korah, men who were in charge of singing in the sanctuary of God. David's name appears in connection with almost half of the Psalms. These authors lived over hundreds of years, and it is clear from the structure of the entire book of 150 psalms that individual psalms were collected over the years and edited in some fashion, updated for place names and some grammar. These psalms were eventually organized into five books, usually labeled 1-5 (e.g., Psalms 1-41 are Book 1, Psalms 42-72 are Book 2, etc.), each ending with a doxology, with the end of Psalm 150 serving as a conclusion to the entire Psalter.

Why were the Psalms written? Many of the psalms began as a poem written out of a very personal situation—a grief, a loss, a celebration, a time of desperation—that was then adapted for congregational use. Psalm 51 is a perfect example of this. Psalms come from all variety of raw experiences and different arenas: "the royal court, priests, Levites, prophets, wise sages, and the poor. And psalms reflect a variety of purposes: to praise, pray, testify, teach, crown a king, etc." These songs that were sometimes composed in dark, private moments of prayer and wrestling were adapted to serve as guides for God's emotional people to express themselves. The God who led these psalm writers through their pain knew that we would live through our own. And so he, the one who shepherds our souls with his Word, gave us an emotional roadmap to navigate life in a broken world.

How can we categorize the Psalms? There are so many different kinds of psalms. While commentators have established a myriad of different systems for organizing the Psalms into groups, in this study we will use the categories described by Dr. C. John Collins, professor of Old Testament at Covenant Theological Seminary. He recognizes nine main categories: laments, hymns of praise, hymns of thanksgiving, hymns celebrating God's law, wisdom psalms, royal psalms, songs of confidence, historical psalms, and prophetic hymns.

How did Old Testament Israel use the Psalms? Unlike the rest of the Old Testament, of which public readings were relatively rare, the Psalms were sung regularly in worship. They were part of temple liturgies, pilgrimages, and public singing. Their scrolls (they were handwritten on some sort of animal skin or parchment that was then sewn together to form one long surface for writing) were placed in the temple to be used by Levitical choirs. The words of regularly used psalms would have made their way into the hearts and minds of the Israelites to such a degree that they informed their prayer life, their imagination, their view of the world. They would have sung them to their children when they were sick and hummed them to themselves while making dinner. The Psalms, for the average Israelite, would have been the only part of the Bible they really knew.

How should we use the Psalms? First, we must remember that the Psalms are poetry, a very different genre from one of Paul's pastoral letters or a book of history like Numbers. And so they lend themselves, like love songs or other music that touches our affections, to shaping our hearts. John Calvin called the Psalms "An Anatomy of all the Parts of the Soul." In them we find ourselves, our experiences, and a way to articulate our feelings to God. But as we use them, we find our words and thinking changed by them. What is a person of faith to say to God as she stares up into the night sky, overwhelmed by the majesty and mystery of what she sees? Psalm 8 helps, giving words to pray and sing back to God. How is a believer to respond when she feels the pull between deeply painful circumstances and her belief that God is always good to his children? Psalm 130 helps articulate these complicated feelings to God, shaping them into a song to sing in faith. Sometimes we as broken people in a broken world have no idea what to say to God in prayer. The Psalms are a rich storehouse for us.

What do the Psalms teach us about talking and singing to God? Laments make up, by some scholars' estimates, up to one-third of the entire Psalter. In the prayer book or song book of the Bible given to us by the Holy Spirit, a huge portion of it is given to expressing our pain, suffering, and need to God. Why do you think this is so? This is a God who wants to hear us, so much so that he gives us fifty different ways of articulating our neediness. As Craig C. Broyles writes, "The laments testify of the value of simply telling our story to God. . . . These laments serve as a reflection on God himself, that he is interested not only in healing but also in pain. Remarkably, they testify that God can be moved. . . . Reflected in these lament expressions is a deity who is not easily shaken or offended and who does not need to be pacified. In other words, he is a God whom we can trust."

The Psalter was Jesus's songbook. He heard these songs as a baby from his parents. He sang these songs as a boy in the synagogue. He prayed these songs as a man when he talked to God. Jesus was shaped by these psalms, so much so that as he hung on the tree and died, the words he spoke were the words of Psalm 22. May we know them and pray them as he did.

Reflection Questions

1. Have you ever read part or all of the Psalms? How would you describe the book?

2. Do you have a favorite psalm? If so, which one?

3. Of all the information you read in the introduction, what did you learn that really stood out to you?

4. What are you hoping studying the Psalms will do for your heart over the next twelve weeks?

Study 2

Tree Planted by Streams of Water

Read Psalm 1

Observation Questions

1. Blessed is the man who does what?

2. What are the descriptions in verse 3 of the man who delights in the law of the Lord?

3. Define with a dictionary the words *righteous* and *wicked*. Define the same words according to this psalm.

Psalm 1 is a wisdom psalm. This category of psalms expands on the themes found in the Wisdom Literature of the Bible like Job, Proverbs, and Ecclesiastes. Psalm 1 may have been written after the first book of psalms (1-41) was finished, to be used as an introduction. It stands here as a gateway to the entire book, boldly inviting us to delve deeply into God's living Word.

Verses 1-2. Who are your people? When something really bad or really good happens, who are the two or three people you tell first? This is what the psalmist wants us to think about initially as he begins Psalm 1. These are the people who have the most influence in your life, who give you advice, help determine how you spend your time and money, affect what you read, watch, and do. According to the writer, these people fall into two categories: the wicked and the righteous. The group we choose determines much about our lives, both in this life and the next. These words, "wicked" and "righteous," can feel puzzling to us at first, as they are not words we normally choose to describe people. They feel exaggerated and absolute, as if only the most evil and the most morally perfect humans deserve these titles. But these are the words that the Scriptures regularly use to describe the two positions we can have in relationship to God: wicked or righteous. The wicked are those who do not belong to the Lord. Their core longing is not to please God but to please themselves. The righteous are simply those who love God and do his will. They live with a readiness to live a godly life. Of course they do not do this perfectly, but the trajectory of their lives is that of obedience. They are called righteous ultimately because of the righteousness of the one to whom they belong.

The psalmist leaves no gray area between the groups nor questions about their future. He clearly describes their fate, beginning with the first word of the first verse—"blessed." "Happy" or "lucky" would also be appropriate translations of this word. But this is not a fleeting feeling. "Blessed" was used repeatedly by Jesus in the Sermon on the Mount to describe the happy ones who would receive various blessings.

So who are these people? According to the psalmist, they are those who avoid the wicked. But who are the wicked? They are the loose, the unattached, the disconnected. They have "cut themselves loose from God's living." They have no moorings or rootedness. They are sinners who miss the mark of God's will for right living over and over again. The happy ones are not tied to the wicked. They do not walk with them, listen to their influence, or become curious about their habits. Neither do they stand with them, toying with evil, trying on the wicked one's ways of thinking and behaving. And they definitely do not sit with them, fully embracing their company, practices, and decisions. The company of mockers are those who blaspheme the Holy Spirit, mock God and his people, and have turned their backs to him.

The lucky ones have deliberately walked away from these mockers, making the choice to belong, instead, with the righteous. Because of this decision, they are described as truly happy, genuinely fulfilled. Instead of filling their hearts and heads with the sinful preoccupations of the wicked, the happy ones are preoccupied with God's instructions.

Torah literally means "instruction," and would have included for the psalmist God's written Word, though at times it referred specifically to certain parts of his Word like the story of the Exodus, the patriarchs, or the Ten Commandments given to Moses. The blessed one spends her time and brain power thinking about all of the guidance given in Scripture. She ponders it, is distracted by it, mulls it over. She is constantly absorbing it, soaking it up like a sponge day and night. This does not necessarily refer to setting aside special time for meditation but to reflecting on God's Word while doing daily, normal activities. It means brainstorming about a verse while doing the dishes. It means repeating a phrase of God's

Word while driving to work until it lodges its way into your mind. It means thinking through each word of a phrase Jesus said while washing your hair. It means memorizing a chunk of Scripture while you fall asleep at night. It is deliberate. It is a choice about what will get your attention when it is not otherwise demanded.

Verse 3. Verse 3 describes the person who plants herself firmly in God's Word like a tree, purposefully planted next to an irrigation stream. Droughts and floods may come and go. The life of this tree is not threatened. It is not immune from living through the normal seasons of life; nor is it a continually blooming, magic tree. But it is protected from debilitating drought, able to withstand otherwise catastrophic conditions because of its proximity to the water. And when the right season comes, in time, it produces fruit. When we plant ourselves firmly in the Word, we are like this tree, weathering trials and struggles. We not only survive, but because of the work of the Holy Spirit in us as he attends his Word, fruit is actually produced in us. Love, joy, peace, good words, repentance —these are the dividends of planting ourselves firmly next to the living water of God's Word. We are rooted, weighty, anchored, tied to his ways and his instructions.

Verse 4. How different is the condition of the wicked! It could not be any further removed from that of the happy, secure person. Unlike the righteous, who are stable and a benefit to others, the wicked are "rootless, weightless, and useless." The image here is that of the wheat farmer who brings his harvest back to separate the food from the useless husks. He would throw an entire pile of wheat up into the air. The heavier heads of wheat would fall back to the ground, while the chaff, or husks, which were lighter, would be blown away by the wind. The wicked are like the chaff— inconsequential, irrelevant, blown away. As George Robertson explains, "Everything they do is time bound and doesn't last."

Unlike the secure rootedness of the righteous one who depends on the Lord, "the self-ambitious, the self-serving, and the proudly self-reliant are like chaff that the wind drives away. . . . Chaff, in contrast to the fruitful tree, has no eternal life, no worth, no stability, no place, and no roots, and cannot endure God's sifting wind of judgment when it blows."

Verses 5–6. The judgment that is referred to here is "the whole of the judicial process by which Yahweh will establish his rule on earth." It is not only the judgment that will happen on the last day but an ongoing process throughout time. The wicked will be alienated by the worshipping congregation, not allowed to be with them. This should give us pause. This is the fate of our friends who do not belong to the Lord. As we read in Hebrews 10:31, it is a dreadful thing to fall into the hands of the living God.

Contrast the distance and shame that the wicked will experience in judgment with the intimate knowing of the righteous. In verse 6 the Lord "watches over," or "knows with approval and affection," those who are his. This is the Hebrew verb *yada'*, which was used to describe the relationship between Adam and Eve that led to Cain. This is profound, deep, historied knowing, like the knowing between a man and his wife. This is the watching over with closeness and tenderness that Jesus describes when he talks about himself as the good shepherd in John 10. In this verse is the only place where we see any action from God in the entire psalm: we learn that the Lord is intimately involved with those who belong to him, that "God's Spirit actively knows, resonates with, and is intimately acquainted with the character and conduct of the righteous."

Here, at the gateway to the entire book of the Psalms, the Lord paints for us a picture of the rooted stability available to his children who choose to preoccupy themselves with his living Word. They are known so personally and secretly by their God. And he invites them to know him in this same intimate way, finding lasting happiness and blessing by meditating on his Word. Will you accept his gentle invitation?

Reflection Questions

4. After reading the commentary, what new information can you add to your definitions and descriptions of the righteous and the wicked? In which category do you see yourself and why?

5. As Christians, and the righteous, we are to be influencers of the wicked, instead of them shaping and influencing us. Where have you found this tension hard for you in the thoughts you have, in your behaviors, or in your interactions?

6. We have this beautiful description of a tree deeply rooted by streams of water, able to endure every type of season, giving us an image of what we are like when drinking from God's Word. Where are you longing to be like that tree?

7. Psalm 1 wants us to be affected by these two vivid images: a deeply rooted, thriving tree versus useless chaff that the wind just blows away. In what areas of your life do you feel like the chaff right now? In what areas do you feel like the tree?

8. In verse 6 the Hebrew word *yada'* is used, which means God knowing us in deep, intimate ways. Do you feel known by him in these ways? Why or why not? What can those sitting around you right now or in your life pray for you to help you connect with this knowing love of the Lord?

Focus verse: *He is like a tree planted by streams of water that yields its fruit in its season, and its leaf does not wither. In all that he does, he prospers.*
Psalm 1:3

Reflections, curiosities, frustrations:

Study 3

Sweeter Than Honey

Read Psalm 19

Observation Questions

1. In verses 1-6, what are some of the things in creation that reveal God's glory?

2. In verses 7-14, what are some descriptions of God's Word and law?

3. Which verse stuck out to you the most upon first reading?

Psalm 19 is considered a hymn of praise, intended to call and enable God's people to praise him for his character and works. It can also be categorized as a wisdom psalm. It celebrates God's law, which to its original hearers would have meant the Torah, the law of Moses, the first five books of our Bible. But first, it asks us to step back from our hurried lives, go outside, and look up.

Verses 1–4a. What we see in the skies is nothing less than the glory of God. The stars, sun, moon, clouds, planets—everything in the "heavens" cannot help but to shout their praise. Day and night they announce the enormity of God and implore us to worship him. The verb translated "pours out" connotes the image of a spring bubbling up, continuously speaking about its creator without any words at all. The 10,000-degrees-Fahrenheit surface of the sun, the 100,000-light-years span of our galaxy, and the 100 billion (at least) stars it contains declare the glory, the weightiness, the extreme importance of God in an unstoppable, silent proclamation. This manifesto cannot be missed. There are no borders that limit its witness. Creation's cry or sound is so pervasive that Romans 1 tells us God has made his existence unmissable: "For his invisible attributes, namely, his eternal power and divine nature, have been clearly perceived, ever since the creation of the world, in the things that have been made. So they are without excuse" (Romans 1:20). This public declaration by nature is part of what theologians typically call general revelation. Everyone can see and hear it, no matter their language or place on the earth.

Verses 4b–6. At a time in history when many of his contemporaries would have been worshipping the sun, David speaks of the sun like a servant. It exuberantly yet obediently travels the course set by its master, returning to its "tent" at night, a simple reference to the sun's night place. Though a servant, it is a capable one from whose

Study 3: Sweeter Than Honey (Psalm 19)

heat nothing on earth can ultimately hide. It seeps its way into the nooks and crannies of every region.

Verses 7–8. Here David transitions us from general revelation to what is called special revelation—God's Word. Just as the sun reveals all of the hidden places of the earth, so God's law reveals and lays bare all of the hidden places of our hearts. There is no hiding from its light. The "law" is a comprehensive term, usually referring to the Torah, that sums up all of God's revealed will. At times it is used to indicate an individual teaching like when God gave Moses the Ten Commandments at Sinai. Other times, like here, it refers to all of Scripture. The overwhelming beauty and grandeur of the created world can only tell us so much: There is a creator who is unbelievably powerful, precise, systematic, and artistic, but what of his morality? And what, if anything, does he expect from humans? Only his Word can answer this and so many other questions. And so in verse 7, David switches from using the Hebrew name El for God, which represents his sovereignty and power, and begins to use Yahweh. This name, which we see translated to "LORD" in most of our Bibles, is the name God uses for himself when he makes covenants with his people. This is the near, personal, knowable God. This God reveals himself in his law, which is refreshing to our souls, reliable in all things, and makes us wise. It is direct, clear, and morally right. It gives spiritual understanding, warns us of pitfalls, and helps us make right choices.

Verses 9–11. Fear means proper reverence. It is the realization that God is God, I am not, and he is in charge. The rule of the Lord leads to purity or cleanliness, which was necessary in the rituals that God's priests would have conducted and that David would have understood. But why does David speak of God's law and his judgments in such fair terms? And what is the connection, if any, between the general revelation of verses 1-6 and the special

21

revelation of verses 7-11? In a word, the connection is structure. There is a structure, an order to our universe. We easily recognize this in the physical world, but there is a moral structure that is just as real. Two hydrogen atoms will always bond to one oxygen atom to form a water molecule unless manipulated. But just as consistent is the fact that if we routinely lie, we will be lied to. Just as sure as the pattern of DNA forming in the shape of a double helix is the principle that showing favoritism among children invites jealousy and rivalry. The moral structure in our world is certain, and the God who created it lovingly and patiently explains in his law how to work with it instead of against it. His law tells us how to run in his world with the wind at our backs instead of against it.

And so it is no surprise that David speaks of God's judgments as precious, as more valuable than anything we could ever earn or buy. They warn us of danger and promise us rewards, or results—good results. Why? Because the creator knows what is good for the created.

Verses 12-14. We come now to the third section of the psalm—David's response. All of the brilliance in the creation along with the goodness in the law brings the psalmist, and us, to a place of vulnerability. This full broadcast of power, beauty, and purity lays us bare. Our faults and brokenness in the face of such things cannot be hidden. We have been found out. David asks helplessly who can see their own unintentional, inadvertent mistakes? We cannot; we are blind to them. As Derek Kidner writes, we cannot see our sin, "not because it is too small to notice, but because it is too characteristic to register." It is so familiar to us, such a part and parcel of our personality, that we don't even notice it. David asks for forgiveness from the sins of which he is ignorant, but he also knows that, like us, sometimes he sins very much on purpose. This term "presumptuous sins" connotes the action of overstepping boundaries in a premeditated way. These purposeful sins are powerful, and David pleads for God to keep him from them, in order that he might be blameless, like an animal without blemish that could rightly be used for a sacrifice. He wants to be innocent, free, clear, acquitted. And so he continues his prayer, asking that Yahweh, the covenant-keeping, near, and knowable God, would make his present life an acceptable one. This must be our prayer as well, as we stare down our own blatant and wilful sin and consider the sin we do not even yet recognize.

The astonishing message for us is that David's prayer was, indeed, answered. The one in whom and through whom all things in the heavens were made, the only one who ever perfectly kept the law, the Word himself, became an acceptable sacrifice. He, the most glorious special revelation, made us pleasing to our Lord, our rock and our redeemer.

Reflection Questions

4. This psalm is called a hymn of praise or a wisdom psalm. Why do you think that is? Where do you see praise and wisdom in it?

5. Because of God's general revelation in creation, no one can miss the work of God. What particular part of God's creation speaks most to you? Why?

6. David describes God's Word, or special revelation, with rich images. Which one resonated the most with you? Why?

7. David transitions from using a name that describes God as powerful and sovereign, El, when describing his creation to calling him a name that shows he is near and knowable, Yahweh, when describing his Word. How have you found this same distinction to be true when you interact with God in creation versus reading his Word?

8. God's Word describes a moral structure to the world as sure as the laws of nature. What about this truth do you wrestle with and find hard to understand? What about it is comforting?

Focus verse: *Let the words of my mouth and the meditation of my heart be acceptable in your sight, O LORD, my rock and my redeemer.*
Psalm 19:14

Reflections, curiosities, frustrations:

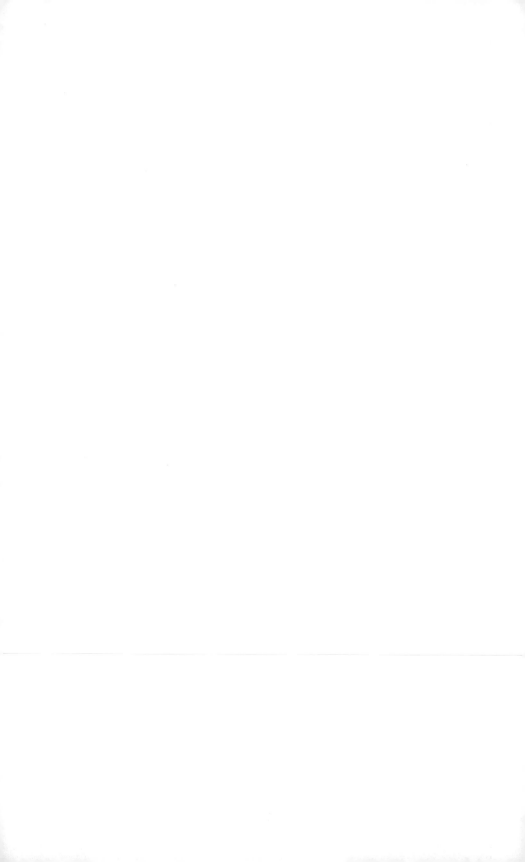

Study 4

Some Trust in Chariots

Read Psalm 20

Observation Questions

1. What things is the psalmist praying the Lord will do for Israel?

2. How many references are made to the "name of the Lord"?

3. What are the things armies trust in when heading into battle instead of trusting in the Lord?

Psalm 20 is a royal psalm, meaning it speaks of the lineage of kings that come from David and how God uses that lineage to bless his people. It clearly foreshadows the Messiah as the only king for whom all of these prayers could completely be answered. In its original context, this is a prayer for the king who is leading Israel out to battle. The king's outcome would be the people's outcome. His victory would be their victory. And so they prayed for God to answer.

This psalm was written for a specific king at a specific time in history, but its true and final fulfillment has come and is coming in the King of Kings, Jesus himself. Therefore, we can read it in its historical context as a prayer for a human king and also as a prayer for God to apply Jesus's work of redemption to our lives as we wait for the fullness of his kingdom to come.

Verse 1. This is a day of trouble. The people are scared and anxious, anticipating war. They are imagining the sons that may die and land that may be lost. Fear grips them as they watch their king (the "you" in this verse) lead the army out to battle, with all of their hopes in his hands. The God of Jacob is the God who led all of Israel out of slavery in Egypt. This story is on David's mind as he writes, reminding himself of the way God had delivered him from days of trouble in the past. "Protect you" is a translation of "place you on high," like being picked up and set upon a rock, protected from danger. As a community, Israel prays for this all-encompassing safety for their king, pleading for the Lord to be his help.

Verses 2–3. The sanctuary was the place of holiness, the place where God dwelt. Sacrifices and offerings were probably made before most military campaigns of Israel, not necessarily to atone for sin, but to ask God to help them in battle (see 1 Samuel 7). These would have been burned on the altar by the priest. This was another way that Israel acknowledged that it was the Lord who would determine the outcome of the war, not their skill or resources.

Verses 4–5. The people of Israel trusted that the king's heart's desire was for their good. They prayed that the plans he had made, literally the "counsel" or "strategy" he had come up with as he prepared for battle, would be successful. They wanted to shout and celebrate when the king returned, knowing that the battle had been won. "Set up our banners" is all one word in Hebrew. It refers to the practice noted in Numbers 2, where each of the tribes of Israel would have had a banner that represented their division. These banners were at times set up, showing each different group as a part of the whole of the nation. Raising them would have signified God's victory over an enemy. The psalmist longs to celebrate with all of the color and regalia of the entirety of Israel.

These are big prayers, prayers that use the imagination of faith and expect that God can answer. Is this how we pray in the midst of trouble? Do we pray for what we are really hoping, or do we hedge our bets? Do we put all of our eggs in the basket of God's ability and listening ear, or do we diversify to protect ourselves?

Verses 6–8. Suddenly there is a shift in David's tone. It almost sounds like he is now on the other side of the battle, having seen his army win. But this is still pre-war. We could translate the first phrase of verse 6, "I have come to the conclusion that the LORD saves his anointed." This is not David's first battle. He has a history with this God, watching him work over and over to deliver. He is convinced that God will hear his people and act on behalf of the king and the army. And he depends on it. In the ancient world, most armies used horses and chariots. But Israel's army was to be different. They were not allowed to acquire many horses and therefore had no chariots either. Imagine coming up against a massive army, the hooves of whose horses you could hear thundering toward you from miles away, while you were outfitted with only a sword, a shield, and possibly a group of archers. David is reminding his people that the Egyptians had plenty of chariots and horses that were effortlessly swallowed up by the sea after the Israelites had safely passed through it. Israel was to trust not in tools or weaponry but in the Lord.

"Trust" in verse 7 may be similar to "proclaim." Other armies boasted in, trusted in, or proclaimed their strength because of their resources or weapons. Again, Israel was to be different. They were to boast in, trust in, and proclaim the name of their God. Is this not what we are called to do in the day of trouble as well? Surely God gives us resources and tools for our own good and use. But our confidence is never to be in those things but rather in the giver of those things. If we are not praying in the day of trouble, chances are we are trusting in something other than God to save us.

Verse 9. One last, urgent prayer is made for Israel's leader. Notice that this is a psalm written by David, given to the people, and prayed for David. David did not face the day of trouble on his own, and neither did the army or the people who waited to hear of the result. When God would answer this prayer, he would answer "us," the collective Israel. They did not face the day of trouble alone, and neither do we. This psalm, while written by David about a human king, is ultimately fulfilled by Jesus, the King of Kings, and all of the requests made about Jesus in this psalm receive the resounding answer from God: Yes!

Look back through the psalm and read it with King Jesus in mind. God has answered us in our day of trouble by doing something about the trouble in a conclusive way. The God of Jacob continues to protect us, hearing Jesus pray for us unceasingly as we fight the spiritual battle that is raging all around us. He does send help, the help of the Holy Spirit, as he applies to us the sacrifice of Jesus. He shapes our hearts so that our desires come more and more in line with his will, and then he grants those desires. He gives us joy and victory, even as we live in this broken world. We do not trust in the tools of this world but in the one who made the tools. All things will pass away, but we will stand and worship when his kingdom comes in its fullness. And so we keep praying. Because the day of trouble is not the final day. We know the outcome of the cosmic battle we are fighting. Death, the last enemy, has been defeated by the anointed king. We call out to him, as the final day of victory inches closer and closer.

Reflection Questions

4. This psalm is filled with big prayers asking for protection and victory as Israel stares down its enemies. Do you pray this way? Why or why not?

5. Israel raised banners as a tangible sign of victories given by the Lord. How do you tangibly acknowledge victories the Lord has given you? Brainstorm some ideas you could try.

6. Imagine coming against chariots and horses and having none, as it was for the army of Israel. Have you ever had to face down such a strong, unmatched force in your own life—at work or in your family or in your own personal story—causing you to have to lean more fully on the Lord? What happened?

7. Israel's enemies were trusting in their weapons for war while Israel was trusting in the Lord's name. What does this look like in your life? Can you give an example?

8. What effect does it have on you when you re-read the psalm with King Jesus in mind? What thought sticks with you?

Focus verse: *Some trust in chariots and some in horses, but we trust in the name of the LORD our God.*
Psalm 20:7

Reflections, curiosities, frustrations:

Study 5

Bring Me Out of My Distresses

Read Psalm 25

Observation Questions

1. What are all the things David is asking the Lord to do for him?

2. What are the phrases David uses throughout this psalm to show his deep emotional distress?

3. Based on verse 19, what are some possible things that David could be struggling with?

Psalm 25 is considered an individual lament, where the psalmist expresses his grief and trouble and asks the Lord for help. It is also an acrostic psalm, much like our acrostic poems. There are seven of these in the Psalter. Each new verse begins with a successive letter of the Hebrew alphabet, with just a couple of exceptions. Though a well-defined structure of themes is hard to find, clearly David is asking for help based on what he already knows to be true about God. David, in his pleading for God to listen, holds God to his word.

Verses 1-3. "I lift up my soul" could also be "I desire" or "I set my heart on." In other words, "I choose you. In the midst of my need, you are the one to whom I speak." And then, in true vulnerability, David pleads, "let me not be put to shame." A few times in the Bible, shame refers to the feeling of embarrassment, like when Paul asks that he would not ever feel embarrassed by the gospel or be ashamed to share it. But this shame is different. This is the fear of being abandoned. David asks, as he begins to fully expose himself and his need to the Lord, "Please, please don't leave me alone. Don't let those around me, especially my enemies, see that I have foolishly been relying on you." But just as soon as he has prayed this, he reassures himself with the truth: "none who wait for you shall be put to shame." Only those who are "wantonly treacherous"—openly dishonest and disloyal—will be abandoned by God. David knows that God is faithful, but David is human, so he comforts himself with the truth that God has already revealed in his Word. David would have known the story of Moses, when God promised to bring his people out of Egypt and be their God, pledging his presence. He would have remembered passages like Joshua 1, where God commanded Joshua to lead Israel into the Promised Land, while encouraging him that he would be with him wherever he went. David applies God's written Word to his own heart, reminding himself that God never leaves his people.

Verses 4-5. What a posture of submission. David, the anointed king, completely humbles himself and asks to be taught. Notice that he does not come with justifications and preambles. Though he clearly knows much—very much—about the Lord, he asks like a child would ask for a skill he desperately wants to learn: "Show me how to do it. Show me the ABCs of obeying you." David does not want to learn only the letter of the law; he wants to understand how to apply it to his life in every way. He seems to understand that a large part of knowing how to do this involves waiting. We may ask God for wisdom about a certain area, child, or relationship and then wait weeks or months before he seems to answer.

David also seems to tell us that most of finding God's will or way has much more to do with his general principles than specific decisions in life. Most of God's will is not mysterious or hidden, like what job to take or who to marry, though these are obviously important decisions. The majority of living out God's will in this life is being willing to submit to what he has already revealed in his Word, to surrender to his authority, to live under his lordship and rule.

Verses 6-11. David again leans on what he knows to be true about the Lord. He uses the Hebrew word *hesed*, which has also been translated "loving-kindness" and "mercy." This love of God is binding, undeserved, and endures forever. Only because he counts on this love can David ask that his many sins, even the sins of his youth, be forgotten. In verses 8-10, David sings out his confidence in the Lord's willingness to show him, a sinner, how to live faithfully. But notice that there is a condition: humility. This is meekness: a deferential spirit that is willing to submit to God's Word, whatever it might say. This is not weakness, a lack of energy, fear, or a lack of strength. It is a right understanding of the real owner of David's life. The more plainly he sees the goodness, steadfast love, and faithfulness of the Lord, the more he understands his need for the pardon of verse 11.

Verses 12-14. These verses allude to something absolutely mysterious and wonderful. The phrase "friendship of the Lord" in verse 14 is actually a Hebrew idiom for "the Lord confides." This "friendship" could also be translated as the Lord's "circle," "company," "council," "fellowship," or "secrets." This is what true intimacy is based on—keeping secrets. And here David is telling us that the God who formed our lungs and the volcanos, the curve of our ears and the curl of the waves, is willing to share his secrets with us. The Lord confides in those who fear him. He whispers to them, entrusting them with truths about his covenant.

Verses 15-21. As we often do in our prayers, David circles back around to subjects he prayed about previously. He is confident that God will protect him. But in that trust, he names all of his anxieties to God. He has enemies both on the outside and the inside. Human enemies hunt him on the outside, but the enemy of his own sin on the inside feels weighty and even frightening. He cries out, asking that God would "guard" his soul, like a gatekeeper or a bodyguard. He knows that against his enemies, within and without, God is his only true protector. He calls upon the innocence and rightness that is his because he belongs to the Lord to preserve and keep him.

Verse 22. This psalm closes with hope yet unfulfilled. David is waiting for God as he ends the psalm. He has voiced all of his concerns and prayed back to God what he knows to be true. And now he waits. This is where we spend most of our lives as believers on this side of heaven; we wait. We lay all of our requests, fears, hopes, anxieties—rational and irrational—and pain in front of the Lord, and we wait. We wait with hope, and we pray with hope for all of the church. Because, as David reminds himself in verse 3, none who wait for the Lord shall be put to shame. None shall ever be abandoned.

Reflection Questions

4. In this psalm David essentially begs the Lord to not leave him alone in his distress, fully exposing his emotional state to God. Do you come to the Lord this way? Why or why not?

5. David comes to the Lord asking him to show him how to follow him, relying on what he has revealed about himself in his Word, and willing to wait on his rescue. Which part of this process is hardest for you: asking the Lord for guidance, studying his Word, or waiting on his reply?

6. David's humility is allowing him to lean into God's loving-kindness to care for all the layers of his distress. How does humility in your life allow you to lean more fully into God's mercy for you?

7. What are your thoughts or response to the commentary on verses 12-14 as it describes this deep "friendship of the Lord" and his entrusting us with truths about his covenant? What deep truth would you most like him to teach you?

8. David repeatedly asks the Lord for help with both the enemies around him and those inside his own head. Which enemies feel the most distressing to you: the enemies around you or the ones in your own mind? Why?

Focus verse: *Turn to me and be gracious to me, for I am lonely and afflicted. The troubles of my heart are enlarged; bring me out of my distresses.*
Psalm 25:16-17

Reflections, curiosities, frustrations:

Study 6

Have Mercy on Me

Read Psalm 51 and 2 Samuel 11:1–12:23

Observation Questions

1. What is the background behind this psalm that is leading to David's prayer?

2. List the things that David is asking God to do for him?

3. How does he describe sin?

Psalm 51 is an individual lament. It is also one of seven penitential psalms, confessional and remorseful in nature, found in the Psalter. David wrote this psalm after Nathan, the prophet, confronted him about his sin with Bathsheba and against Uriah. This is David, the man after God's own heart, the mighty and righteous king of Israel, the musician who wrote scores of praise songs to God. But this is also David the human who struggled, as we all do, against his own pride, lust, selfishness, and arrogance. David, who genuinely loved God and loved Israel, had been living for months in self-deception. He walked around under the weight of his unconfessed sin, unwilling to deal with or oblivious to his own guilt. Then, in his kindness and mercy, "the LORD sent Nathan to David," as we read in 2 Samuel 12:1. This confrontation was God's gift, to lead David to repentance. In that one moment of recognition, David saw the weight of his sin. But through Nathan's words to him, "The LORD also has put away your sin; you shall not die" (2 Sam. 12:13), David saw the weight of God's mercy. Out of that experience came this psalm, which millions across the ages have used for their own prayers of repentance.

Verses 1–2. David knows that he is coming as a beggar, with nothing in his hands but his own culpability and regret. He appeals to God's covenant love, asking him to "blot out" what he has done as one would wipe or rub a name out of an ancient book. He has gone from being blind to his own sin to seeing it as multifaceted and complicated. He lists here the ways he has wronged God. "Transgressions" refers to rebellion, "iniquity" to an inner twistedness, crookedness, or perversion, and "sin" to missing the mark. David has a clarity now about just how dirty his heart is. He wants not only to do a ceremonial washing like a priest; he wants to be scrubbed, like a 1920s woman working her laundry on a washboard. It is like he is comparing himself to "a foul garment, needing to be washed and washed."

Verses 3-5. This sin of his, though he had been trying to hide it from himself, constantly accused and confronted David. Can you imagine his turmoil and distraction every day as he tried to live with the shame and guilt of what he had done, keeping it hidden, pressing it down within himself in order to stay in denial? Every day it was in the forefront of his mind, taunting him, ridiculing him. Isn't this what our sin does to us? It shames us, guilts us, convinces us there is nothing to be done about it, that there is no relief, no dealing with it. And the longer we keep it hidden, the more damage it does. David knows that his sin has offended God, the true God of the covenant. With his statement in verse 4, he is not denying the damage he did to Bathsheba or Uriah or others but rather declaring that it is the true God that he has ultimately wronged.

Notice that David does not treat this incident as an outlier or some anomaly, as if it is not representative of his heart in general. He goes on, in verse 5, to explain that from the very moment of conception, he was sinful—not that his mother was sinning when she conceived, but that his soul was dark and amiss from its creation. The outbreak of anger and evil demonstrated by David taking Bathsheba for himself and then killing Uriah did not suddenly appear because of something Bathsheba did. Her bathing on the roof was simply the occasion for the sin that already festered in David's heart. Is this not true of us? We may believe that we have tamed the selfishness and corruption of our own hearts, right up until some precipitous event shows us the wickedness lying just under the surface in our souls. True for us, as it was for David, this is not a punishment. To be shown our own sin is the mercy of God leading us to repentance.

Verses 6-7. David understood that it is not just the outer actions with which God is concerned; he wants purity on the inside. And so David uses the imagery of the tabernacle and sacrifice to plead with God that he might be made clean in a lasting sense. Hyssop was an herb in the mint family that grew prolifically in the Middle East. The Israelites would have used it almost like a paintbrush to mark their doorposts with lamb's blood when the angel of death passed over them just before they escaped from Egypt. Later, in the time of the tabernacle, priests would use hyssop as a symbol of cleansing when lepers or other unclean persons had met the requirements of purification. David knew that his sin had made him unclean, separated from God and unable to do anything about it. He wanted to be readmitted, like the lepers, clean, purified, able to access God again.

Verses 8–9. David certainly had not known joy and gladness while hiding his sin, especially around the sanctuary. Every encounter with God or anything holy would have felt heavy and complicated, a reminder of his guilt. Verse 8 could be translated, "let the bones that you have broken dance." He longs for the joy that he freely felt in the past to be restored to him. But he knows it can only come with forgiveness. Again he pleads with God to "blot out" the record of his sin written in God's book.

Verses 10–11. Here come the beloved words we know so well from this psalm and the many tunes written for it: "Create in me a clean heart, O God." The word "create" here is the same Hebrew verb used in Genesis 1:1, "In the beginning, God created." David does not simply ask for his heart to be set back to where he was before his affair and murder; he asks for God to start from nothing, to start over, to construct an entirely new heart. Commentator Derek Kidner notes, "With the word 'created' he asks for nothing less than a miracle." David knows this is what he needs—a miracle. He needs God to reach into him and bring to life what is dead, and then to sustain him in that life. Verse 11 is not a reflection of David's fear that he has lost the Holy Spirit or his eternal security. Here he is talking about the ability to live a holy life. This is a man who knows very well his own weakness and frailty. He knows the only way he can live in obedience is by the Spirit.

Verses 12-14. "Ways" in verse 13 probably means God's ways with sinners, the way God counts us righteous because of the sacrifice. For David this would have meant the sacrifice offered by priests in the tabernacle, over and over. For us, it means the sacrifice offered once for all by Jesus, the ultimate High Priest. David knew the joy and relief he would experience when forgiven for this terrible, burdensome sin would be huge. It would lead him to tell other people about the way that his God dealt with filthy, guilty people— by accepting a sacrifice in their place.

The "bloodguiltiness" in verse 14 probably refers to Uriah's murder. And again, David speaks of the kindness of God, as he mentions God's "righteousness." It is presumably God's own righteousness or goodness that he gives to us sinners that David speaks of here.

Verses 15-17. It is not that David is contradicting God's law by saying God does not want any sacrifices. He means that performing the ceremony without a changed heart does no good. What God wants is a repentant, remorseful heart. As Kidner writes, "The best of gifts is hateful to him without a contrite heart. . . . God is looking for the heart that knows how little it deserves, how much it owes."

Verses 18-19. There is always a relationship between the spiritual health of individuals and the spiritual health of all of Israel, and therefore, all of the church. The two cannot be separated. Repentance breeds repentance. And a worshipping community of people with humble hearts can effect change in their community and beyond.

This adulterer and murderer found his way, by God's mercy and a bold prophet, to repentance. Whatever we have done, the same God summons us by his loving-kindness to come, see all of the many complicated layers of our sin, agree with him in his judgment, and be restored to joy by his forgiveness.

Reflection Questions

4. David describes sin and the effects of sin in detail in this psalm. Do you feel similar or different than him about it? Why?

5. David knew the darkness of the sin in his own heart that was right below the surface. When have you experienced your sin surfacing and it surprised you? What happened?

6. David knew the depths of his own weakness and frailty, literally asking God to make him a new, flawless heart. Do you feel the same despair and need with your own heart? Why or why not?

7. Describe how you feel when you have been forgiven for a specific sin. What is your response toward God? What is your response toward others?

8. How would you describe the act of repentance to a non-Christian? What does repentance feel like? What is its result?

Focus verse: *Purge me with hyssop, and I shall be clean; wash me, and I shall be whiter than snow. Let me hear joy and gladness; let the bones that you have broken rejoice.*
Psalms 51:7-8

Reflections, curiosities, frustrations:

Study 7

My Soul Thirsts for You

Read Psalm 63

Observation Questions

1. How does the psalmist describe his desire for God?

2. What does he say results when he remembers God and meditates on him?

3. What does he say will happen to those who are seeking to harm him?

Psalm 63 is an individual lament. As with most individual laments, its author lays down a complaint, declares his confidence in God's ability to intervene, and looks forward to worshipping him for the work he will do. David is thought to have written this psalm while in the wilderness of Judah, when he fled Absalom in 2 Samuel 15. He was, as he had been multiple times, running for his life, this time from his own son. He was in the desert, a dry, desperate, barren place. Of course he was thirsty. But for what? Here we will see that David challenges us to deeper devotion and intimacy with God. He had come to a place in his life where his primary thirst, the longing that haunted him and moved him, was not his thirst for water but for Yahweh, the Lord himself.

Verse 1. This is Yahweh, the God who enters into a relationship with his people and guarantees it by his Word. This is the knowable, near God. David is not searching for someone of whom he is unsure. As Derek Kidner explains, "The longing of these verses is not the groping of a stranger, feeling his way towards God, but the eagerness of a friend, almost of a lover, to be in touch with the one he holds dear."

All humans experience this thirst, though most do not recognize it for what it is, a spiritual thirst. Jesus talks about this in John 4, when he tells the woman at the well that the water she gets from the well will leave everyone thirsty for more. But he offers living water, which can truly satisfy. For those of us who know the Lord, we are immediately convicted by David's purity of heart. He is, at this moment, clear about his soul's ache. He is not distracted by the beautiful things in this world for which we often reach to satisfy the constant longing we feel for something more, something deeper, something glorious. In this parched, arid, lonely desert, David wants the presence and favor of God even more than he wants water. As Tim Keller says, "The favor of God is at least as important to the soul is as water is to the body. There is a thirst that is only satisfied by worship." David fully recognizes and is content with the fact that what he truly craves is a person. But how did he get to this point?

Verse 2. David has seen glimpses of God's glory. He has tasted his goodness, and he cannot stop himself from wanting more. This encounter happened for David over and over in the sanctuary. In the act of worship, in the place of obediently singing and offering sacrifices to God, David had, in a sense, fallen in love with God. And now, stripped of all comfort, privilege, and safety, his appetite for God is even stronger.

Where has this happened for us? For those of us who are believers, most have at some point caught a glimpse of the true greatness, majesty, and splendor of God. This glory haunts us. We may have first seen it in a worship service, as we sang and heard his people give testimony about him. We may have heard of it in stories told, in the reading of the Word, in the taking of Communion. We hear echoes of it in beautiful music, see flashes of it in a sunset, a mountain, the sea. And we always want more. But do we ignore the ache? Or do we, like David, keep seeking for more?

Verses 3–4. David has reached the pinnacle of contentment with God alone. For him, the steadfast and abiding love of God is the highest good. For David, keeping that love is worth everything. And so in the midst of his awful circumstances, he sings. Here David shows us one of the keys to obedience, no matter our mood, status, or prospects. He does physical things to affect himself spiritually. He moves his body to bend his soul. He opens his mouth and sings, and lifts up his hands to worship. He leads his inside with his outside. Notice that nothing has changed circumstantially, but in an act of obedience, David leads his heart by moving his body.

Verse 5–8. "Fat and rich food" is literally "marrow and fat." This is an idiom, and it is a metaphor for "the joy, greatness, and beneficence associated with the love of the Lord." God's kindness is like a feast that satisfies our souls. David responds to the feast with more singing, more praise. There is a back and forth, an active response by David to his anticipation of God's answer. His longing for God is not short-lived; in fact, it continues for days. The "watches of the night" is a military guard idea referring to the breaking up of a night into three sections of four hours each. While others were sleeping, David was awake. For hours. But instead of brooding about Absalom or worrying about the future, he rehearses the history he has with the Lord. He meditates on God's faithfulness in the past, which leads him to continue to name God as his source of help and protection in the here and now. David, the mighty king, finds comfort in God as he sings, like a baby bird under its mother's wings.

"My soul clings to you" could also be read "my soul follows hard after you." Remember, again, that no circumstance has changed. David is still in the desert, still being chased by people who want to kill him. But he will not let go of God, even as he believes that God is the one ultimately not letting go of him.

Verses 9–11. David speaks here of the futures of those trying to kill him. By sight, at this point, they were winning. He was, of course, the one hiding out in the desert. But by faith, David predicts their demise, and their ultimate judgment by God. They will be killed by the sword, leaving their bodies as food for wild animals. For David this is not hateful or angry speech, just fact. This destruction is imminent for the enemies of God.

This king is God's king. Once justice has been done, more praise will come to the God who saved. The mouths of the faithless will be shut, while those who have trusted in the true king will sing all the more.

It is possible for us, weary, distracted pilgrims, to read this psalm and only be discouraged, standing far off from David in awe. We hear him trusting, praising, worshipping even in the midst of worse circumstances than ours. We take stock of ourselves, complaining, ignoring God, feeling apathetic, maybe even cursing him. The message of this psalm is not shame, judgment, or condemnation for those of us who have not come to David's level of clear devotion. Instead, the Spirit speaks to us here and reminds us that we too feel the longing for God. We too, even in this moment, know the ache for more. Jesus would say to us what he said to the woman at the well in John 4: "Everyone who drinks of this water will be thirsty again, but whoever drinks of the water that I will give him will never be thirsty forever. The water that I will give him will become in him a spring of water welling up to eternal life" (John 4:13–14). The love of God that David could not resist is no less available to us. Let the psalmist's quest and reach for God encourage us to keep following hard after Jesus, whose love is better than life.

Reflection Questions

4. David describes God satisfying his deepest thirst and longing when he is in crisis. Has worshiping God when you are in crisis helped? Why or why not?

5. How would you define God's glory? How and when have you personally seen it displayed?

6. In the midst of this awful circumstance David decides to sing to God, which changes everything. What behaviors or rituals do you do that help your heart catch up to your head and reconnect to God despite your circumstances?

7. Instead of brooding about Absalom or worrying about the future, David rehearses the history he has with the Lord. What currently are you worrying and brooding over? What parts of your history with the Lord can you spend time thinking on instead?

8. David's own son is after him (can you even imagine?), and yet the only thing that will satisfy is more of the Lord. Why does intimacy with God have more of an emotional draw for David than being able to reverse this situation with his son? Does that surprise you?

Focus verse: *O God, you are my God; earnestly I seek you; my soul thirsts for you; my flesh faints for you, as in a dry and weary land where there is no water.*
Psalm 63:1

Reflections, curiosities, frustrations:

Study 8

Because He Knows My Name

Read Psalm 91

Observation Questions

1. List the action words that describe what the Lord will do for the psalmist.

2. List the specific things the Lord will deliver the psalmist from.

3. In verses 14-16, the speaker changes from the psalmist to the Lord speaking. Rewrite those verses in your own words.

Psalm 91 can be categorized as a song of confidence, which allows God's people to express their trust in him even in dark and difficult circumstances. It is also a wisdom psalm. The author is unknown, though some have suggested Moses. We know neither the context nor the occasion for the writing, but we can be encouraged by its application to the life of anyone who belongs to the Lord.

Psalm 91 walks us through all manner of danger, assuring us that God is in control of every circumstance and that he uses even pain for our good. The instability of this world is real and engenders massive fear in us. But as Sinclair Ferguson has preached, "There is a fear that can deliver us from all other fears—the fear of the Lord." Ferguson goes on to say that the fear of the Lord acts like a medicine, permeating to the roots of all our other fears. Here the psalmist takes our eyes off our circumstances and focuses them on the only one we need to fear—the Lord himself.

Verses 1-4. Before teaching us about what we should believe, the psalmist speaks of his own experience with God. He has made his home under the covering of El Shaddai. The Lord has been his haven and hiding place, his sanctuary and escape. And he will persuade us that the Almighty can be those things to us as well.

Verse 3 shifts voice, and the author starts to instruct us about this God. Unlike some other places in Scripture where the "you" employed is plural, "you" in verse 3 is singular. This is an intensely intimate and personal kind of protection that is both tender and strong. "The fowler," or hunter, is a metaphor for unexpected evil plots of others, including Satan. "Pestilence" represents disease or deadly plague. We are protected from these dangers, both seen and unseen. We are covered like baby birds by the careful wings of a mother bird, shielding her young from sun, rain, and predators. God's care for us is tender. But we also have a wall, a guard and barricade that is his firm and reliable commitment to us. His care is for us is strong.

Verses 5-8. The psalmist goes on to the next set of dangers. For those who struggle with anxiety, common fears of the day can magnify into huge, terrifying monsters at night. We have no control over sickness that surreptitiously enters our households and the beds of our children. War, heat, famine—none are under our command. The psalmist assures us that we need not fear any of these things. Even though we see a thousand others die right next to us, we will be kept safe. In fact, not only will we be secure, but we will eventually see the wicked punished. Because we abide in the Lord, no evil will come to us.

But wait a minute, you may be thinking. Evil does come to us in many forms. Friends die, parents get cancer, spouses have affairs. Is the psalmist lying to us? The next verses invite us to take a step back and see that while evil persists, it is only a tool in the hand of the one who both began and will finish a good work in us.

Verses 9-13. The key phrase in verse 10 is "shall be allowed." Events in our universe, including even our everyday circumstances, are not haphazard or purposeless. Evil and suffering that come into our lives have been allowed by our Father to discipline and train us, to deepen our joy and our intimacy with him. He is not surprised by the terrible phone call or the doctor's bad report. All has been authorized by the Almighty. And while physical suffering is inevitable, our souls and salvation are untouchable while under the care of God. Sometimes this is comforting. Sometimes, if we are honest, it makes us question God's goodness. And so we must read on.

Believe it or not, one of the jobs of the angels is to protect the children of God. Matthew 18:10 and Hebrews 1:14 both tell us that these heavenly beings are sent to serve those who will inherit salvation. We may never know the number of times we have been saved from tragedy by one of these mighty spiritual beings. Even the lion and the snake, symbolic of the most physically dangerous creatures, cannot harm us unless God allows it. And therein lies the key. God does allow suffering, but it is suffering with a purpose, directed by the hand of a benevolent, protective Father, who has already written the glorious end of the story. God never wastes our pain.

Consider the ultimate sufferer, Jesus. When tempting him in the wilderness, Satan tried to twist verses 11-12 of this psalm to cause Jesus to act presumptuously by testing God. But Jesus understood that his Father's love for him would not preclude his pain but would employ it for good. And in fact, God did not send his angels to spare Jesus from the cross. Instead, as Ligon Duncan points out, "He sent those angels to minister to him in the garden to prepare him for the cross." God himself suffered, that we might not be alone in our suffering. And not only that, he utilizes our suffering for our own benefit. Romans 8:28, which tells us that for those who love God all things work together for good, is ultimately true. We do not know the timing, and we may not see the redemption of our suffering until the new heaven and the new earth, but we have been promised that we will see it.

Verses 14–16. But why? Why would the creator give such amazing, individualized attention to me, one small life among billions? Because I was good? Because I successfully controlled my anxiety? Because my faith was strong and I read, taught, or sang his Word? No, the Lord himself answers in verse 14, as the voice of the psalm changes once more: "It is only because he clings to me, knows me, and depends on me." The Hebrew verb here is *yada'*, "to know." But this is biblical knowing, like the way Adam knew his wife and therefore conceived Cain. This is an intimate knowledge. Because of the way you cling to me, says the Lord, I will deliver you.

What will this deliverance look like? Like an ear that listens for his child's voice in the midst of the crowd. Like answers in the form of practical help. Like immediate or eventual rescue. It will look like God's presence, like him being next to his children when they are stressed, scared, or otherwise in trouble. It means that whatever suffering is allowed into their lives, God will walk through it with them. And in the end he will rescue them in the ultimate way, giving them "long life," probably referring to eternal life. The final and most decisive danger, death itself, is not to be feared by the one who clings to the Almighty.

Reflection Questions

4. Psalm 91 is a song of confidence and a wisdom psalm. Define *confidence* and *wisdom* and write why you think this psalm fits into these two categories.

5. The psalmist transitions from telling the ways the Lord has been his hiding place to speaking to us as to how the Lord will be our refuge in each of our individual lives. Of the long list of things the Lord will protect you from, which one stuck out to you the most or made you wrestle and feel confused?

6. Suffering will come, in all kinds of forms, leaving its mark, and yet God promises not to waste it, to remain present and engaged with us in it, and to transform us through it. Is this comforting to you? Why or why not?

7. It's remarkable to think that Satan used this psalm, the Word of God, to lie and try and tempt Jesus in the wilderness. In what ways currently is Satan using lies or misrepresenting the Word of God to you? What effect is it having on your life?

8. This deep, intimate knowing of the Lord, or *yada'*, is what ultimately leads to deliverance over and over again for the psalmist. What do you think this type of intimacy with the Lord looks like? How does it differ from your current relationship with him?

Focus verse: *Because he holds fast to me in love, I will deliver him; I will protect him, because he knows my name.*
Psalm 91:14

Reflections, curiosities, frustrations:

Study 9

Come, Sing to the Lord

Read Psalm 95 and Exodus 17

Observation Questions

1. What are the first few verses of this psalm calling us to do?

2. What does it say are in God's hands or are formed by his hands?

3. In verses 8-11 of this psalm, what did the Israelites do to God and what resulted?

Psalm 95 is a prophetic hymn, which means that it contains themes talked about by Old Testament prophets like covenant faithfulness and listening to God's voice. This psalm has been used by Christians consistently since the fourth century to call themselves to worship. We almost get the picture of the psalmist walking down the path surrounded by the houses of Israelites and calling into their spaces as he goes, "Come! Let us go sing! Come with me into God's presence!" This psalm has, in fact, through the ages, simply gone by the Latin name, the Venite, which means "Come." It is a summons to us, an invitation to be shaken from our apathy, distraction, idolatry, and anxiety and to refocus our attention onto the sovereign one who both shepherds and warns us.

Verses 1–2. The writer summons Israel to the sanctuary, where worship would have happened. He calls them, and therefore us, to an unabashed, loud, joyful noise. This means boisterous in-tune singing and out-of-tune singing, calling and responding, well-played instruments and out-of-sync drums. It means joy and celebration, like the energy of a pep rally, the crescendo of a holiday *Messiah* sing-along. It is all of that energy, chaos, order, and intensity. As Derek Kidner writes, "Before making ourselves small before him, we greet him here with unashamed enthusiasm as our refuge and rescuer . . . indeed we address one another, to make sure that we rise to the occasion, not drifting into his courts preoccupied and apathetic."

Preoccupation and apathy are our baseline. We, as humans, often live in a place of ingratitude. In order to worship, we must lean against this familiar space. If we only worship when we feel like it, there will be very little worship indeed. We must discipline ourselves to worship and be thankful. Thirty-eight times throughout the Bible God commands us to sing. These verses tell us how to start.

As Tim Keller says, "Worship is ascribing ultimate value to something in such a way that engages your entire being." This is what the psalmist is calling us to in these first verses. This is not a call to half-hearted, perfunctory duty. It is a summons from the only person whose worship will not distort our souls. The reality is, we all worship something. These verses call us to transfer the value we have put on created things onto its rightful owner.

Verses 3-5. The first people who sang this psalm lived at a time when most of the people surrounding them believed in multiple gods, each controlling a certain sphere of the world. These words at that time were absolutely countercultural. They claim one God above all others and then go on to explain the extent of his rule—boundless. Unlike other gods, Yahweh actually made, and therefore is in charge of, every part of the earth. Here creation equals dominion. The repeated mention of "his hand" signifies God's authority. This God said to the oceans of the earth, "Thus far shall you come, and no farther; and here shall your proud waves be stayed." This God "commanded the morning" and "caused the dawn to know its place" (Job 38). This God is in charge.

Verses 6-7a. Now the psalmist calls us to a different tone. There is a progression of loud exuberance and joy followed by reverence and awe. We are given three directives, one right after the other: "worship," "bow down," and "kneel." And while we bend our bodies in obedience, the aim is to shape our hearts in humility. But why? Why should we come, sing, or bow? The psalmist answers us in verse 7: because he is our God. He is not some far off deity that we must appease in order for our crops to grow. In fact, this absolutely unlimited superintendent of all things likens himself to a shepherd, and us to his sheep. He is a caretaker, guide, and protector. Jesus gives us a clearer picture of this in John 10 as he describes the good shepherd as the one who goes as far as to lay down his life for the sheep. The mighty creator takes the humble place of a shepherd. Our response must be to humble ourselves before him. He has taken the initiative, as God always does, of loving us. We must answer his love with our worship.

Verses 7-10. Suddenly the tone changes. As James Montgomery Boice explains, "Abrupt changes like this are not infrequent in the psalms, and the warning to hear the voice of God and obey it is actually a critical part of what needs to be said about the worship God accepts." This is still the voice of our loving shepherd. But good shepherds, along with cuddling, leading, and gently encouraging, also lead their sheep away from danger.

So what is the warning about? The psalmist is referring to Exodus 17, where the Israelites got angry with Moses because there was no water to drink in that particular part of the wilderness. Moses named that part of the desert Massah, meaning "testing," because they tested the Lord with their grumbling, and Meribah, meaning "contending." Well, they were thirsty. Didn't they have the right to be mad that there wasn't any water? In this case, we must understand the bigger story. God had just brought all of Israel out of Egypt in a miraculous way. There had been plagues, then the Passover, then the Egyptians giving the Israelites their gold on their way out, then the parting of the Red Sea followed by the constant presence of God in the cloud and the fire. God had clearly shown himself over and over as able to provide for, protect, and rescue Israel. They should have trusted him by then. But instead they "quarreled," "grumbled," and were ready to stone Moses. Their memory was that short.

Notice that this is not a case of Israel not following the rules or worshipping some hunk of wood or gold. For forty years God "loathed," or was disgusted with, that generation. Why? "They have not known my ways" (verse 10). As one commentator writes, "We must be clear here that the reason for this judgment stems not from Israel's refusal to live by a moral code but from their fundamental misunderstanding of Yahweh himself, exhibited in distrust that Yahweh would remain true to 'the people of his pasture' and provide water for 'the flock under his care.'" It's not that they ignored the Ten Commandments. They didn't trust God. They didn't know him. They didn't lean into him, expect from him, wait on him, gamble on him. He had promised to be their God, but when their outer circumstances looked different than their expectation of the promise, they believed their eyes, not God's Word. They started with fear and discouragement, slid into discontentment and anxiety, and made their way to quarreling and grumbling.

Are we so different from these Israelites?

Verse 11. This generation refused to take God at his word. Their consequence was exclusion from the Promised Land. This is where the psalm ends. It is a stark warning, meant to wake us up to the ever-present possibility and temptation of sliding into a skeptical hard-heartedness that refuses to trust God.

But there is hope. This is not the last word written about the warning of this psalm. Hebrews 4 quotes this psalm multiple times. It informs us that this warning was not only for the Israelites singing and hearing the psalmist. It is also for us. "Today if you hear his voice, do not harden your hearts." "Today" is right now. "You" is us. Hebrews 4:8-10 reads, "For if Joshua had given them rest, God would not have spoken of another day later on. So then, there remains a Sabbath rest for the people of God, for whoever has entered God's rest has also rested from his works as God did from his."

The rest that the Israelites would have known had they trusted God and made their way to the Promised Land is available to us. It is not the physical land of Canaan, but more than that. The physical rest that had been promised to Israel pointed to something much more—a deeper, spiritual rest. It is the Sabbath rest of God, the enjoyment of Jesus's finished work of redemption. It is salvation. The message for us in the worship and warning of Psalm 95 is summarized for us in Hebrews 4:11: "Let us therefore strive to enter that rest, so that no one may fall by the same sort of disobedience."

Reflection Questions

4. This psalm has been known as the Venite, or "Come," which means to move or travel toward. How has reading this psalm caused your heart to move or travel toward God?

5. This psalm calls us to push against apathy and preoccupation in order to worship even when we don't feel we want to. What is currently causing your apathy and preoccupation when it comes to worshiping the Lord? What happens when you start to sing and worship God even when you don't feel like it?

6. It was countercultural at the time to think of there being one God, instead of multiple gods controlling the world. Although that is different at this point in history, what are some idols or gods that compete in your heart versus the one true God?

7. Where currently are you, like the Israelites in this psalm, skeptical or hard-hearted toward the Lord? What are the reasons for this?

8. In what ways have grumbling, quarreling, and anxiety contributed to you currently struggling to hear God's voice and enter into his rest?

Focus verse: *Oh come, let us worship and bow down; let us kneel before the LORD, our Maker!*
Psalm 95:6

Reflections, curiosities, frustrations:

Study 10

Bless the Lord

Read Psalm 103

Observation Questions

1. Define the word *praise*.

2. According to this psalm, what are all the things the Lord has done for you?

3. What does he do specifically with our sins?

Psalm 103 is categorized as a hymn of praise. It was written by David but is not tied to any specific event in his life. A psalm for all people, it has been loved and utilized by believers for hundreds of years as a tool to rouse their affections and respond to the one who is worthy of praise.

Verses 1-2. Some psalms begin by speaking to God's enemies, some to God's people, and others to God. This psalm begins with the author speaking to himself, to his own soul. He recognizes in his heart apathy, slowness, and lack of right response to who God is. And so he talks to himself. He commands his soul to "bless the Lord," to pay homage, salute, acknowledge, and bow to God. In fact, David uses a literary device often used in the Bible called an *inclusio*. He repeats the first line of the psalm in the last line of the psalm, creating a pair of bookends that signal to us what everything in between is really about—awakening our hearts, souls, and minds to praise the promise-keeping God, Yahweh.

As humans living in a disappointing, broken world that is so often not the way it's supposed to be, we tend to focus on our immediate pain or sadness, busyness, or routine. It is so easy to become totally immersed in the daily arduous task of just getting through life that we, frankly, forget about God. We go about our days and overlook his goodness, usually not consciously, hour by hour, task by task, until the entire day has gone by and we realize we have not even spoken to or acknowledged the Lord.

As one commentator warns, "The opposite of praise is forgetfulness." Forgetting God's goodness is not only easy; it is the habitual posture of our hearts unless some intervention occurs. Here is where we find help from David; he self-diagnoses his forgetful, ungrateful heart, and he commands it to worship. This might feel disingenuous, as if all true praise must be spontaneous. This is false, and just another way for Satan to subtly distance us from our sustainer. Impromptu worship is wonderful, but it is rare when we are busy or distracted by circumstances. This is why we must, as David does here, speak to our own souls, and command them to sing to God. But why? What are the benefits we enjoy as his children? And how do we "forget them not"?

Verses 3–5. We rehearse them. We list them for ourselves. We count our blessings one by one, as the children's song goes. David lists for himself some of the benefits he has known of his God. The biggest? Forgiveness. Mentioned in verses 3 and 4, redemption from sin always has to do with someone's blood in the Old Testament. There was—and is—no forgiveness of sins without the spilling of blood. For David this would have meant the killing of animals in the sacrificial system established in the book of Leviticus after the Exodus. But that system always pointed to something more, the ultimate sacrifice by the perfect and spotless one, Jesus himself. For us, remembering this benefit might look like imagining Jesus during his last week of life and how he endured terrible things for us. It might look like singing a favorite hymn out loud that speaks about his forgiveness. It might even look like, when talking to God, choosing to repeat back to him part of your history with him and the many times he has forgiven you.

Though it is the greatest benefit, forgiveness of sins is not the only thing David mentions. He speaks of healing us from our diseases, which could be literal sicknesses. More likely, this is a metaphor for "adversities or setbacks." We remind ourselves that when we make it to the other side of these, it is the Lord that has gotten us there.

And there are still more benefits. We sin, and continue to sin. Instead of humiliation or condemnation, what we get is a crown and unending love. We deserve punishment and curses. Instead, as David reminds us in verses 4 and 5, God's response to us is his devotion and his mercy, which reinvigorate us.

Verses 6-10. David continues to heap up perk after perk by referring to a story of absolutely stunning kindness on God's part. This is what he is referring to in verses 6 and 7. The setting was the desert shortly after God had rescued his people from slavery in Egypt. Moses had gone up on the mountain to receive the Ten Commandments. In the meantime Israel had made for themselves a golden calf and had begun to worship it as God. Moses had asked to see God's glory. While he was not allowed to see God's face (because no one could see the face of God and live), God put him in a gap in the mountain, covered him with his hand, and passed by, letting Moses see only his backside.

So, when asked directly to see his glory, what about himself did God reveal? What aspect of his character did he choose to make abundantly clear? Verse 8 of our psalm is what God declared as he passed by Moses. Exodus 34:6 is almost directly quoted: "The Lord, the Lord, a God merciful and gracious, slow to anger, and abounding in steadfast love and faithfulness." God describes himself this way many other times in Scripture. In fact, this verse is repeated so many times in the Old Testament that James Montgomery Boice writes, "It almost becomes a credal statement answering the question, 'what is God?'" This is what the God of Israel wants us to know about him, and what we need to remind ourselves about. This is how he wants to be defined: generous, accommodating, long-suffering, benevolent. Unlike humans, who love to hold a grudge, he does not stay angry. Though he may display his wrath, his mercy is greater. Is this what we believe about God when we think of our most shameful sin, the one that brings us the deepest regret? Is it possible for us to take this doctrinal statement, this declaration God makes about himself throughout the Old Testament, and apply it to that dark place? This is just one more reason to bless the Lord. Because whether we believe it or not, he has chosen to treat us with compassion.

Verses 11–16. David continues by describing God's kindness in three ways. In verse 11 it is bountiful and great. In verse 12 it is decisive and firm. And in verse 13 it endures. In verse 14 "frame" could better be translated "form." Our creator understands that we are finite, and he knows our limits better than we do. It is no surprise to him that we are so needy. We are transient, like the grass and the flowers in verse 15. Our hope is in the fact that God is familiar with our fragility and vulnerability and that it causes him to have compassion on us.

Verses 17–22. The impermanence of our lives is contrasted with the permanent love of God, whose compassion is passed from us to our children and to their children. His throne is secure, and his kingdom is boundless. He is worthy of praise, not just from us, his people, but from every part of creation. And so David goes on to instruct the angels in heaven to praise him. These, who always obey, who always adhere to his will, must praise him too. Unlike us, his wavering people, the angels do not have to be convinced, cajoled, or aroused to praise. These "hosts" are his army, his trained ones. They are those who "do his will" (verse 21). Finally, David calls on "all his works" to bless the Lord. As Abraham Kuyper said, "There is not a square inch in the whole domain of our human existence over which Christ, who is Sovereign over all, does not cry, Mine!" Each blade of grass, every valley and mountain, each star and planet, every creature and ocean is called to thank, extol, and honor the Lord.

David ends by commanding his soul, one last time, to bless the Lord. This is how we must talk to ourselves, to our souls. We must train them to rehearse the true things about God. We must force ourselves to sing. These songs and remembrances are our weapons against spiritual depression, discontentment, and apathy. We must direct our hearts to sing, especially when we do not feel like doing so. We must plead with our souls and awaken our hearts to bless the Lord and forget not all his benefits.

Reflection Questions

4. The posture of our hearts is to go about our days and overlook his goodness unless we call our soul to praise. Does calling your soul to praise feel forced or disingenuous? Why or why not?

5. David's praise involves listing all the benefits of knowing the Lord. Which thing on his list has the most impact on you? Why?

6. This statement is repeated over and over in the Old Testament and in this psalm about the Lord: "The Lord is merciful and gracious, slow to anger and abounding in steadfast love." Rewrite this doctrinal statement in your own words.

7. We are needy, transient, and vulnerable, while God's kindness is bountiful, firm, enduring, and well aware of what we are. Which part of your humanity do you most resist? Which part of God's kindness do you most crave?

8. The angels, all of creation, and we are commanded to sing to the Lord recounting all that he faithfully does. Write three or four sentences of your own "praise" and "song" to him, recounting what he has done specifically for you.

Focus verse: *For as high as the heavens are above the earth, so great is his steadfast love toward those who fear him; as far as the east is from the west, so far does he remove our transgressions from us.*
Psalm 103:11–12

Reflections, curiosities, frustrations:

Study 11

The Lord Will Keep You

Read Psalm 121

Observation Questions

1. List the things that the psalmist says the Lord will keep from harming you?

2. Does the Lord sleep?

3. Define the words *keeper* and *guardian*.

Psalm 121 is a song of confidence. It is also a psalm of ascent, one of about fifteen psalms that were probably sung by the Jews as they made their way to Jerusalem three times a year for their designated religious festivals. The trip to Jerusalem for these pilgrims was literally a trip of ascent, since Jerusalem was geographically the highest point in the region. They would have walked together in large groups, singing these memorized psalms together with friends, relatives, and children as they went. Sung every year along the way, these songs must have become like old friends—familiar and comforting. Once in the spring, once in the early summer, and once each autumn, all of the monotony of daily life was left behind. Thoughts, songs, eyes, and hearts were all directed toward a common goal of the festival. Daily tasks were exchanged for worship, renewal, and reminders of who their God was. Jesus walked these roads to Jerusalem and sang these psalms along the way. This was probably an antiphonal psalm, meaning different lines of the song were sung by different groups of singers. It would have had the effect of a call and response, like two groups of people talking to each other through music.

Verse 1. As the writer made his way with the crowds of pilgrims traveling to Jerusalem for one of the prescribed festivals, at some point looking toward Jerusalem would have meant looking up, toward the hills and mountains. It is tempting to read the first two lines of this psalm as one phrase, as if the psalmist refers to the hills as his place of help. But a good translation separates the lines: I lift up my eyes to the mountains. Full stop. And what do I think and feel about them? An Israelite on pilgrimage probably would have first felt fear. All sorts of thieves and other dangers hid out in the hills. They were good cover for evildoers who laid in wait for travelers. While their goal, Jerusalem, was amidst those hills, the ascent would have naturally prompted the question in the next line: Who can help me?

This was the ultimate question for the Israelite pilgrim. But it is the decisive question for us as believers who are also pilgrims in this foreign land. Where will we go for help when we face threats and danger? We want to consistently go to God. But we waffle. We wander. We find solace in a myriad of other created things. We tend to focus on the danger instead of the rescuer. This is our struggle as we say to Jesus, like the father of the boy in the gospel who needed healing, "I believe; help my unbelief" (Mark 9:24). And so we need to preach to ourselves and to others the truths we find in the rest of this psalm.

Verses 2-4. The Lord, who made heaven and earth, was set apart from the other gods in the psalmist's time by this sweeping claim of creation. Other supposed deities were believed to have a specific and narrow range of influence in the world. For example, Dagon, whose image bowed down to the ark of the covenant in 1 Samuel, was a god of water and grain. Baal, the Canaanite god, was in charge of the sun, weather, and fertility. In a bold claim of limitless, unfettered power, the psalmist sets his God apart as the one who created the mountains and all things. While other gods took long naps (see Elijah and the prophets of Baal, 1 Kings 18:25–40), the creator God never sleeps. This ever-vigilant God actually pays attention to pilgrims. Notice the repetition of the word "keep" in verses 3-5. Its word family includes *watch*, *preserve*, *charge*, *careful*, *attend*, and *guard*. In fact, this word is used eight times throughout the entire psalm. Remembering that Hebrews used repetition to draw our attention to things, think about those eight times. The architect of the cosmos watched and guarded Israel on pilgrimage, not just as a nation, but as individuals. How did he keep them? First, he steadied them, as steadying feet on loose stone and treacherous grades.

Verses 5-6. Second, the Lord gave refreshment through his presence and emotional encouragement. The language here speaks of both the dangers of sunlight by day and moonlight by night. The blistering sun of the Near East was a real threat to the traveler who had no place to take cover in the heat of the day. Heatstroke was dangerous and possible. And so the Lord is a shade, a refuge from the burning sun. As for the moon, ancient writers sometimes would refer to a state of overwhelming emotional distress as "moonstroke" or lunacy, which they thought was caused by the moon. Today we would probably call this mental illness. But even this cannot ultimately harm the pilgrims.

Notice the way that the author names the two opposites of the day and night, signaling something to the original audience. Naming these two opposites was a Hebrew writing technique that expresses completeness or the whole of a thing. There is nothing unguarded by this God, nothing over which he does not keep watch. As sojourners who long for the new heaven and the new earth, this song, sung by thousands of Israelites, is also our song. This same God keeps our footsteps, stays awake while we sleep, refreshes us, and acts as our shield and guard.

Verse 7. This is the climax statement of the psalm: "The Lord will keep you from all evil." Totally. Without exception. This sweeping statement gives us pause. Alarms are triggered in our minds and hearts as we think of the evil that *did* come to the Israelites as they traveled and *does* come into our lives. Babies die, diseases ruin bodies, broken relationships tear families apart, entire countries endure famines. We could all make individual lists of very real and specific evil that we have seen or experienced.

Even with this declaration of keeping us from evil, the psalmist is not claiming an exemption from pain, struggle, or even death. What the writer knows is that there is an evil worse than any conflict, person, or circumstance. It is more ruinous than agony or death itself. Indefinite separation from God is the ultimate evil; it is the worst thing that can happen to us. It is the ultimate trouble.

And of this we can be sure: God keeps the psalmist, and us, from this terminal evil. The one who built the world never takes a break from attending to us. There is no exception, pause, or lapse in his care. And therefore there is not a moment when we can be disconnected from him. Instead, his presence, attendance, and attention is as real as the mountains the psalmist is considering.

Verse 8. Every moment and every place, this is where God will accompany us. But God doesn't promise an easy life in this psalm. As Derek Kidner writes, "In the light of other scriptures, to be kept from all evil does not imply a cushioned life, but a well-armed one." God's attendance means his presence, his Word, his blessing on us, a full cup and table in the presence of our enemies. Jesus made this same seemingly conflict-ridden claim of protection amid trouble. In Luke 21:16-18 we read of Jesus predicting his disciples' future as he says, "You will be delivered up even by parents and brothers and relatives and friends, and some of you they will put to death. You will be hated by all for my name's sake. But not a hair of your head will perish. By your endurance you will gain your lives." He plainly tells them that some of them will die. And yet they are protected. How? Their spiritual integrity and the state of their souls cannot be touched, because they cannot be separated from God.

This is the absolute freedom and security we have as God's children. Nothing can touch us! Not in an ultimate, conclusive, decisive way. No pain, circumstance, or anything of this world can do real and lasting harm to us. As Eugene Peterson writes, "Faith is not a precarious affair of chance escape from satanic assaults. It is the solid, massive, secure experience of God who keeps all evil from getting inside us, who keeps our life, who keeps our going out and coming in from this time forth and forevermore." The pilgrim's journey to Jerusalem is a parable for all of life. And on that journey, God's keeping of us is more secure than the foundation of the hills themselves.

Reflection Questions

4. This psalm is one of the fifteen psalms of ascent that were memorized and sung at important festivals for the Israelites. What do you think the benefits of memorizing and singing these as a community gave God's people? Does your current church have traditions like this?

5. Ask yourself the same question that the psalmist asks as he looks around and suspects danger, "From where does my help come?" What is your gut response to this question? What truths do you use to remind yourself that God is your help?

6. The word "keep" is used eight times in this short psalm to communicate God's watchfulness and care for his people. What effect, if any, did the repetition of this concept in the psalm have on you? Have you felt this watchfulness of God over you in your life?

7. The naming of the two opposites, sun by day and moon by night, shows the full spectrum of God's care and watchfulness over all destructive, harmful things in our life. What is currently going on in your life causing you to need this truth?

8. This reflection on this psalm summarizes its truth down to one statement: No pain, circumstance, or anything of this world can do real and lasting harm to us. Does this thought fit with your current thinking about the effects of pain and trauma in your story? Why or why not?

Focus verse: *The LORD is your keeper; the LORD is your shade on your right hand.*
Psalm 121:5

Reflections, curiosities, frustrations:

Study 12

Shouts of Joy

Read Psalm 126

Observation Questions

1. Four times in this psalm the Lord is mentioned. What are the descriptions of him?

2. How many times is the phrase "shouts of joy" used? What does it mean?

3. Define the words *sow* and *reap*.

Psalm 126 is a community lament. While individual laments are a conversation between a single, struggling person and God, community laments are a more public, communal occasion. In this psalm, the people of God cry out together in their anguish, acknowledging their ache for God to show up and do something about their broken and heart-wrenching circumstances. It is also a psalm of ascent.

Verses 1–3. According to 2 Kings 25, Nebuchadnezzar, the king of Babylon attacked Jerusalem in the late sixth century BC, eventually burning the entire city, breaking down the city walls, and taking the majority of the population into exile. The captain of the guard left a small portion of some of the poorest of the land to be vinedressers and farmers. By 586 BC, the city was completely destroyed. For decades, the people of Judah lived in Babylon, having lost all hope of returning to their homeland, the land promised to their ancestors by their God. No longer could they worship at Solomon's magnificent temple in Jerusalem, the center of Jewish culture, nor sing their songs, nor celebrate the festivals commanded by God. They were a captive people, a nation without a homeland.

But when Cyrus, king of Persia declared around 538 BC that the Jews must return to Jerusalem and rebuild the temple, hope broke out. Suddenly those from the tribes of Judah and Benjamin, along with priests and Levites, were headed back to Jerusalem by the thousands, along with the temple vessels that Nebuchadnezzar had taken in the siege of Jerusalem (see Ezra 2). It was like a dream. It was surreal, unbelievable. As the pilgrims walked the miles back to their lost city and began to see familiar landmarks, emotion must have overwhelmed them. They celebrated, shouting, laughing, a great multitude of joy, a throng of wonder. It was the unexpected bliss, the unleashing of a sudden blessing that took them by surprise and filled their mouths with laughter. And the nations around them noticed.

These are the memories that the psalmist is rehearsing in his mind as he walks the miles toward the city of Jerusalem. He recalls the rush of elation and the tears of joyful unbelief that Israel had known as they were reunited with their homeland.

Verse 4. Suddenly the tone changes. The psalmist stops mid-memory and asks the God who filled their mouths with laughter to act again, to surprise them. Israel has returned, but to broken walls and a decimated temple. Looking at a desert wadi where dust and earth stretch out for miles, it would seem completely unlikely that a river could ever exist in such a place. And yet that is exactly what happens when the clouds break in the Negeb. Looking at their desolate city with its broken walls, the returned Israelites must have felt like it was silly to hope for the fullness of life in Jerusalem that they had enjoyed before the Exile. There is reason for hope, but also a lot of work to be done.

Isn't this often our experience? We've seen God act in the past. We have stories about his faithfulness to our families and to us individually. But that was then, and this is now. And today the way forward looks intimidating, hopeless, overwhelming. We, like the psalmist, must remember how God has shown up again and again. And we must plead with him to amaze us with his mercy one more time. We must, as George Robertson teaches us, "be defiant" in our hope. We cannot allow cynicism to creep in and tell us lies about God's intentions for us.

Verses 5-6. Planting time was one of anxiety and uncertainty. A farmer's entire investment was placed in the ground in faith. He patiently sowed the seed, putting the future of his children in the soil. He had no control over weather, pests, success, or failure. It was a time of trust and vulnerability. But the time of bringing in the crops was one of profit and return, celebration and plenty. The same one who slowly and patiently labored with no guarantee of success returns with arms full, rejoicing as he comes. The writer knows that only God can bring the yield. And only with the God of unexpected miracles are dry places "potential rivers."

Looking at the broken places of our lives, it often seems ludicrous to hope that some sort of redemption could happen in what seem to be such hopeless circumstances, damaged relationships, unending grief. But God. But God makes the clouds break in the Negeb. But God turns the heart of a king and commands a return to the homeland. But God turns a tiny seed into arms full of food for everyone. We can focus our eyes on our own poverty, or we can fix our eyes on the one who can do all things. As Eugene Peterson writes, "We can decide to live in response to the abundance of God, and not under the dictatorship of our own poor needs." The way of joy is a defiant hope in the one who has acted for us in the past, and "joy is nurtured by anticipation." It is the release of all that we have to the Lord's control, trusting that the way he has been kind to us in the past is a template for the way he will show kindness to us in the future. As God's children, our lives are, "bordered on one side by a memory of God's acts and the other by hope in God's promises, and who along with whatever else is happening are able to say, at the center, 'We are glad.'"

Reflection Questions

4. Psalm 126 is a community lament. Think of a recent situation where you, individually or as a community of believers, laid your trouble before the Lord in prayer? What resulted?

5. Under Nebuchadnezzar and Cyrus the Jews experienced the extremes of bondage and freedom. What impact do you think that had on their prayer life and view of God? How can you relate?

6. When you feel fearful, overwhelmed, and intimidated about your current situation, how often do you use stories of God's faithfulness in your past to shape your view about your current reality? How could you practically work on using these memories as a source of encouragement to draw on?

7. The psalmist asks the Lord to restore them as he has done in the past. This requires hoping in the Lord to act. What about hoping feels risky to you?

8. Twice the psalmist describes sowing tears to bring about a crop of joy. Where do you currently need to sow in tears to the Lord? What would the crop of joy look like?

Focus verse: *He who goes out weeping, bearing the seed for sowing, shall come home with shouts of joy, bringing his sheaves with him.*
Psalm 126:6

Reflections, curiosities, frustrations:

Study 13

Read Psalm 130

Observation Questions

1. In what state is the psalmist coming to the Lord?

2. What is he waiting for and hoping in?

3. Define what a watchman does.

Psalm 130 is a psalm of ascent and an individual lament. It is also a penitential psalm, one of seven found in the Psalter. These psalms seem to outline in the Old Testament the doctrine of justification by faith, or the pronouncement that we are treated as right with God because of something he has done, not because of anything we could do. Because of this, Martin Luther called them the Pauline psalms, as Paul in the New Testament would keep coming back to the theme of justification by faith. Scholars argue about when exactly this psalm was written, but its application is timeless, as we shall see.

Verses 1-2. This man has been undone by his own sin. At some recent point, he has seen the darkness, ugliness, evil, and danger of his sin. Maybe he knew about sin, in a definitional sense. Maybe he has repented before, has been aware of how he has offended God, has known the implications of his guilt, and has even made some sort of sacrifice to atone for it. But this has all been head knowledge. In this moment he feels the horror of how evil his heart truly is. He is drowning in this awareness, overwhelmed by the full realization of his heart's corruption. These are the depths, the sinking, helpless, shocked places. In these places there is no time for pretense or cover up. Only desperation is appropriate. In his anguish, he cries out to God, begging that he would listen, knowing he has no right even to ask for God's ear.

Have you ever reached this point? The point where you clearly see the wretched darkness of your heart and its hatred, evil, greed, or pride? It can feel utterly hopeless, especially if it is a sin you have battled against repeatedly. Has God given up on you? Are you losing in the struggle against sin? These are the questions that can plague us in these moments. Here is the answer the psalmist gives: Absolutely not. When we feel that God gives us clarity about our sin, what we should actually feel is hope. Why? Because seeing our sin plainly is a mark of growth, an indicator of maturity. The more clearly and truly we see God in all of his glory, the more despicable our sin will look to us. As Eric Alexander says, "It is natural that the nearer you get to the light, the more ugly the blackness seems." God, of course, is not surprised by our sin like we are. He knows our going out and coming in, every thought we have, every motivation and twisted agenda. It is only for us that these realizations are shocking.

Verses 3–4. This is the gospel expressed in the Old Testament. If God started keeping track of our sin with the intention of judging it, none of us would stand a chance. After we've clearly seen our sin, the logical next step is to wonder what God, a holy God, will do to us because of it. Notice that this is not a recent convert writing the psalm. This is someone who knows God and has known him for some time. Consider others who have prayed this way. David, the king, prayed desperately in Psalm 51 for forgiveness and a new heart when he saw the evil in his own. Isaiah was undone by his sin in Isaiah 6 when he clearly saw the holiness of God. These are giants in the story of redemption, and they were taken aback by what they saw in themselves. God's forgiveness was their only hope.

God's forgiveness is still our only hope when we realize the weight of our sin. Even that one sin that you've given up fighting, that you're ashamed to name out loud. With God, there is forgiveness for that one. What God has given us in these verses is a free pass to admit what we are: sinful, broken, frail. There is no need to posture before him as if he doesn't know what we're hiding. We sin; he forgives. This is part of why we fear God, as verse 4 tells us. Only he can complete this transaction of forgiveness. Only he, the Creator, the one who knows all hearts, makes the decision to deliberately take on the problem of sin. The animal sacrifices the author of this psalm would have known were only a shadow of his ultimate solution, the terrible transaction of his innocent son for us, his guilty created ones.

Verses 5–6. The psalmist knows that what he really longs and waits for is not just relief from the guilt of his sin, but for the Lord himself. "His word" probably refers to some specific words of Old Testament prophets about how God promises to be with and restore Israel to himself. It refers to some sort of saving act by God. The verb used here that is translated "wait" has these terms in its word family: twist, stretch, tension. This is physically what waiting feels like. We want to strive. Our bodies and minds fidget and twist, eager to do something, anything, to force God to act. We wait for our sins to be forgiven, for our prayers to be heard. We wait for God to provide our daily bread. We wait to hear from God about our doubts. We wait, like watchmen. As Eugene Peterson writes, "A watchman is a very important person, but he doesn't do very much." The watchman would have stood all night, probably on the wall of the city, alert for any danger. But mostly he waits for dawn. And so we, too, wait, eager for all sorts of salvation to come, just as the watchman strains his eyes, eager to see the first streaks of daylight.

Verses 7–8. The psalmist has come full circle. He began in the depths, unnerved by the weight of his sin, but he has talked himself to a place of trust and confidence. Derek Kidner writes, "Nothing could be further than the shut-in gloom and uncertainty of 'the depths' than this. The singer is now liberated from himself to turn to his people and to hold out hopes that are far from tentative." This is how God works, isn't it? He assures us of our forgiveness, and we cannot help but to want to reassure other people, when they are overwhelmed by their sin, that he will do the same for them. It is the character of God that the psalmist is resting in here. His steadfast love is covenant love. It is, as Sally Lloyd Jones writes, the "Never Stopping, Never Giving Up, Unbreaking, Always and Forever Love." And what he does, how he acts, what he cannot help but accomplish, is redemption, the definition of which is "the action of saving or being saved from sin, error, or evil." It is who he is.

But the second definition of redemption is this: "the action of regaining or gaining possession of something in exchange for payment, or clearing a debt." This writer, emboldened by what he knows about God's wide mercy and "plentiful redemption" is exhorting Israel to hope in him. We have a much fuller picture than the psalmist had. We know the particulars of that redemption. We know the shape and cost of that payment. And therefore we put our hope, all of our hope, in his Word. God gained possession of us in exchange for Jesus. The salvation the psalmist waited for has come, and is coming. Put your hope in him.

Reflection Questions

4. Have you ever realized the depth of the sin and darkness in your own heart? What made you realize it?

5. What sin do you most frequently try and hide from God? What could thinking on his forgiveness do to change that?

6. We all know the tension of waiting. What are you waiting on the Lord for when it comes to a particular recurring sin?

7. The psalmist says he waits for the Lord more than the watchman waits for the morning or dawn, which he knows is coming. Do you wait for the Lord in the hard areas of your life as if he is actually coming?

8. Which part(s) of the two definitions of *redemption* made the biggest impression on your heart in regards to your recurring sin? Why?

Focus verse: *My soul waits for the LORD, more than watchmen for the morning, more than watchmen for the morning.*
Psalm 130:6

Reflections, curiosities, frustrations:

Acknowledgments

Hope: To Ray, thank you for loving me well everyday and always pushing me to look for the silver lining. To my children, Cana, Thea, and Nias, love you guys so much, thanks for being you. To my parents, thank you for always giving me unconditional love and hours of listening. TCU Sisters, you are always on the path with me walking beside me, daily, near or far, for twenty years. I am beyond lucky to have you. To my Austin and SA sisters (you guys know who you are), you are the most supportive cheerleaders and always know what to say when I get overwhelmed—love you! Jen Hinriches...you da best. To Renae, the best editor a girl could ask for, whose processing over Voxer this go around has been especially rich and enjoyable. Jacob, you are the best publisher in the world, and we are so spoiled to have you! Chris, I love you...can you believe we get to do this together? The Lord is kind!

Chris: To Elsa, thank you for your excellent editing help. I hope you never stop writing. To Marcia, you are my God-given cheerleader. Hope, Jacob, and Renae, you are an example of God doing immeasurably more than I ever would have thought to ask.

A Note on Sources

So many writers, professors, and pastors have influenced my writing about the Psalms. Some have been specific conversations about pressing questions. Others have been general impressions and lenses for psalm study that have led me in one direction or another. In particular, I am indebted to Mark Dalbey and his willingness to spend an entire plane ride from St. Louis to New York City in January 2018 answering my questions about suffering. And to Tim Keller, whom I cornered in March 2018 at a conference at Sea Island, Georgia, to ask about the definition of "evil" in certain psalms. I have drawn from C. F. Keil and F. Delitzsch's Psalms commentary (http://biblehub.com/commentaries/kad/psalms/1.htm), C.S. Lewis's *Reflections on the Psalms* (Harcourt Brace, 1958), and Derek Kidner's Psalms commentary (Tyndale Old Testament Commentaries, InterVarsity, 1973). I have also drawn heavily from Monergism.com and their excellent library of sermons, especially those of George Robertson, Eric Alexander, and Sinclair Ferguson.

Notes

1. Introduction to the Psalms

5   "when sung in faith": Collins, "Introduction to the Psalms," 939.

6   "the royal court": Broyles, *Psalms*, 1–2.

6   He recognizes nine main categories: Collins, "Introduction to the Psalms," 940.

7   "An Anatomy": Calvin, "Author's Preface."

8   "The laments testify": Broyles, *Psalms*, 33.

2. Tree Planted by Streams of Water: Psalm 1

12   This category of psalms: Collins, "Introduction to the Psalms," 940.

13   "rootless, weightless, and useless": Kidner, *Psalms 1–72*, 49.

14   "Everything they do": Robertson, "Truly Happy Person."

15   "the self-ambitious": Waltke and Houston, *Psalms as Christian Worship*, 141.

15   "the whole of the judicial process": VanGemeren, *Psalms*, 83.

15   "God's Spirit actively knows": Waltke and Houston, *Psalms as Christian Worship*, 142.

3. Sweeter Than Honey: Psalm 19

20   Psalm 19 is considered: Collins, "Introduction to the Psalms," 940.

22   "not because it is too small": Kidner, *Psalms 1–72*, 100.

4. Some Trust in Chariots: Psalm 20

28   Psalm 20 is a royal psalm: Collins, "Introduction to the Psalms," 940.

29   They prayed that the plans: Kidner, *Psalms 1–72*, 102.

5. Bring Me Out of My Distresses: Psalm 25

36   Psalm 25 is considered: Collins, "Introduction to the Psalms," 940.

36   "I lift up my soul": Study note on Psalm 25:1, *ESV Study Bible* (Wheaton, IL: Crossway Bibles, 2008), 967.

38   The phrase "friendship of the Lord": VanGemeren, *Psalms*, 269.

6. Have Mercy on Me: Psalm 51

44   "a foul garment": Kidner, *Psalms 1–72*, 90.

46   Later, in the time of the tabernacle: VanGemeren, *Psalms*, 437.

46   "With the word 'created'": Kidner, *Psalms 1–72*, 192.

47   "The best of gifts": Ibid., 193, 194.

7. My Soul Thirsts for You: Psalm 63

52   "The longing of these verses": Kidner, *Psalms 1–72*, 224.

52–53   "The favor of God": Keller, "God, Our Intimate Friend."

54   "the joy, greatness, and beneficence": VanGemeren, *Psalms*, 490.

8. Because He Knows My Name: Psalm 91

60   Psalm 91 can be categorized: Collins, "Introduction to the Psalms," 940.

60	"There is a fear": Ferguson, "When Fear Takes Shelter."
62	"He sent those angels to minister": Duncan, "Shadowed."

9. Come, Sing to the Lord: Psalm 95

68	Psalm 95 is a prophetic hymn: Collins, "Introduction to the Psalms," 940.
68	"Before making ourselves small": Kidner, *Psalms 73–150*, 344.
69	"Worship is ascribing ultimate value": Keller, "Worship."
70	"Abrupt changes like this": Boice, *Psalms*, 778.
70–71	"We must be clear here": Broyles, *Psalms*, 374.

10. Bless the Lord: Psalm 103

76	"The opposite of praise": VanGemeren, *Psalms*, 756.
77	More likely, this is a metaphor: Ibid., 757.
78	"It almost becomes a credal statement": Boice, *Psalms*, 836.
79	David continues by describing: Study note on Psalm 103:11–13, *ESV Study Bible* (Wheaton, IL: Crossway Bibles, 2008), 1068.
79	"There is not a square inch": Kuyper, Inaugural address, 488.

11. The Lord Will Keep You: Psalm 121

86	"moonstroke": Peterson, *A Long Obedience*, 35.
87	"In the light of other scriptures": Kidner, *Psalms 73–150*, 432.
87	"Faith is not a precarious affair": Peterson, *A Long Obedience*, 41.

12. Shouts of Joy: Psalm 126

93   "be defiant" in our hope: Robertson, "One Thing I Do Know."
94   "potential rivers": Kidner, *Psalms 73–150*, 440.
94   "We can decide to live": Peterson, *A Long Obedience*, 93.
94   "joy is nurtured by anticipation": Ibid., 95.
94   "bordered on one side": Ibid., 98.

13. More Than Watchmen: Psalm 130

101   "It is natural that": Alexander, "Psalm 130."
102   "A watchman is a very important person": Peterson, *A Long Obedience*, 138.
102   "Nothing could be further": Kidner, *Psalms 73–150*, 447.
102   "Never Stopping, Never Giving Up": Jones, *Jesus Storybook Bible*, 36.
102–03 "the action of saving": *Oxford Dictionaries*, s.v. "redemption," https://en.oxforddictionaries.com/definition/us/redemption.
103   "the action of regaining": Ibid.

Works Cited

Alexander, Eric. "Psalm 130, Part 1." Sermon. Monergism.com. http://tapesfromscotland.org/Audio5/5761.mp3.

Boice, James Montgomery. *Psalms (An Expositional Commentary). Vol. 2, Psalms 42-106.* Grand Rapids, MI: Baker Books, 1996.

Broyles, Craig C. *Psalms.* New International Biblical Commentary. Peabody, MA: Hendrickson, 1999.

Calvin, John. "Author's Preface." In *Calvin's Commentaries— Complete.* Christian Classics Ethereal Library. https://www.ccel.org/ccel/calvin/calcom08.vi.html.

Collins, John C. "Introduction to the Psalms." In *ESV Study Bible*, 935–41. Wheaton, IL: Crossway Bibles, 2008.

Duncan, Ligon. "Shadowed." Sermon, June 28, 2008. http://ligonduncan.com/shadowed-711/.

Ferguson, Sinclair B. "When Fear Takes Shelter: Psalm 91." Sermon, First Presbyterian Church, Columbia, SC, August 17, 2011. https://www.sermonaudio.com/sermoninfo.asp?SID=719121529251.

Jones, Sally Lloyd. *The Jesus Storybook Bible.* Grand Rapids, MI: Zondervan, 2007.

Keller, Tim. "God, Our Intimate Friend: Psalm 63." Sermon. Monergism.com. http://media1.wts.edu/media/audio/psc02_copyright.mp3.

———. "Worship: Psalm 95." Sermon, Institute for Christian Worship Lectures, July 7, 2002. http://resources.thegospelcoalition.org/library/tim-keller-sermon-on-worship-psalm-95.

Kidner, Derek. *Psalms 1-72.* Tyndale Old Testament Commentaries 14a. Downers Grove, IL: InterVarsity Press,

1973.

———. *Psalms 73–150*. Tyndale Old Testament Commentaries 14b. Downers Grove, IL: InterVarsity Press, 1973.

Kuyper, Abraham. Inaugural address at the dedication of the Free University. In *Abraham Kuyper: A Centennial Reader*. James D. Bratt, ed. (Grand Rapids, MI: Eerdmans, 1998).

Peterson, Eugene. *A Long Obedience in the Same Direction: Discipleship in an Instant Society*. Downers Grove, IL: InterVarsity Press, 1980.

Robertson, George. "One Thing I Do Know: Psalm 126." Sermon, First Presbyterian Church, Augusta, GA, January 10, 2010.

———. "The Truly Happy Person: Psalm 1." Sermon, First Presbyterian Church, Augusta, GA, July 10, 2005. https://firstpresaugusta.org/resource/the-truly-happy-person/.

VanGemeren, Willem A. Psalms. Vol. 5, *The Expositor's Bible Commentary*. Rev. ed. Grand Rapids, MI: Zondervan, 2008.

Waltke, Bruce K., and James M. Houston. *The Psalms as Christian Worship: A Historical Commentary*. Grand Rapids, MI: Eerdmans, 2010.

Other At His Feet Studies

We pray that you will continue to sit at the feet of Jesus, studying his word. To help you with this, we have also written Bible studies for women on these books of the Bible:

Romans (28 studies)

1 Samuel (16 studies)

Philippians (12 studies)

Printed in Great Britain
by Amazon